Muscle Cars

BY DENNY VON FINN

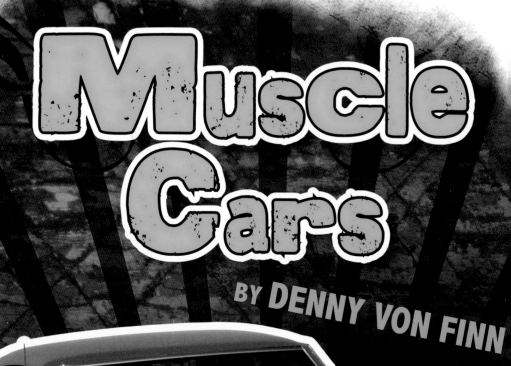

TORQUE™

BELLWETHER MEDIA • MINNEAPOLIS, MN

Are you ready to take it to the extreme?

Torque books thrust you into the action-packed world of sports, vehicles, and adventure. These books may include dirt, smoke, fire, and dangerous stunts.

WARNING: READ AT YOUR OWN RISK.

This edition first published in 2010 by Bellwether Media, Inc.

No part of this publication may be reproduced in whole or in part without written permission of the publisher. For information regarding permission, write to Bellwether Media, Inc., Attention: Permissions Department, Post Office Box 19349, Minneapolis, MN 55419.

Library of Congress Cataloging-in-Publication Data
Von Finn, Denny.
 Muscle cars / by Denny Von Finn.
   p. cm. — (Torque. Cool rides)
 Includes bibliographical references and index.
 Summary: "Amazing photography accompanies engaging information about muscle cars. The combination of high-interest subject matter and light text is intended for students in grades 3 through 7"—Provided by publisher.
  ISBN 978-1-60014-272-7 (hardcover : alk. paper)
 1. Muscle cars—United States—History—Juvenile literature. 2. Muscle cars—Pictorial works—Juvenile literature. I. Title.
 TL23.V645 2010
 629.222—dc22
                                2009008483

Text copyright © 2010 by Bellwether Media, Inc. TORQUE and associated logos are trademarks and/or registered trademarks of Bellwether Media, Inc.

Contents

What Is a Muscle Car?

A muscle car is a two-door passenger car. It has room for a driver and three to four other people. The most famous muscle cars were built from 1964 to the mid-1970s.

Muscle cars are the quickest vehicles American automakers ever made. These high-performance cars are named for their powerful engines.

The **Big Three** (Chrysler, Ford, and General Motors) fitted these light cars with large engines. They were the first affordable cars to have **large-displacement** engines. A light car with a large engine has a good **power-to-weight ratio**. This makes the car much quicker.

Muscle Car History

John DeLorean is often given credit for making the first muscle car. He was a young **engineer** at General Motors in the early 1960s. His team knew that lots of young people wanted fast, cheap cars. They offered the mid-size Pontiac LeMans with a larger engine. This car was called the GTO. It came out in 1964. Lee Iacocoa was also working on a muscle car at this time. This legendary muscle car was called the Ford Mustang. It came out in 1964.

Fast FaCt

American Motors Corporation made many muscle cars in the 1960s and 1970s. These included the Javelin and AMX.

Muscle cars became less popular in the 1970s. Gasoline became more expensive. Smaller cars offered better **fuel efficiency** than muscle cars. New safety laws also made quick muscle cars expensive to drive.

Automakers have reintroduced updated muscle cars. The Dodge Charger, Dodge Challenger, and Chevrolet Camaro are new muscle cars. They share **design cues** with early Chargers, Challengers, and Camaros.

Muscle Car Parts

The most important part of a muscle car is its engine. A muscle car has an engine with eight **cylinders**. It is called a **V8** engine. The cylinders are arranged in the shape of a "V."

One of the most famous engines ever used in muscle cars was the **Hemi**. The Hemi was built by Chrysler. It was named for its *hemi*spherical **combustion chamber** in each cylinder. Chrysler introduced a new Hemi engine in 2002.

Muscle cars also feature rear-wheel drive. This means the engine uses a **drive shaft** to give **torque** to the back wheels. This helps give muscle cars their power and quickness.

Fast FaCt

A 1970 Dodge Charger can accelerate quickly. It can go from 0 to 60 miles (97 kilometers) per hour in 5.5 seconds!

Muscle Cars in Action

Classic muscle cars have great **straight-line speed**. They were very popular among drag racers in the 1960s and 1970s. In the 1960s, Ford offered several muscle cars built for drag racing.

Today, car shows are the best
place to see classic muscle cars. **Mint**
examples of classic muscle cars are rare.
These vehicles sell for hundreds of
thousands of dollars at auction.

Fast FaCt

In 2006, Barrett-Jackson auctioned two Plymouth Hemi Barracuda muscle cars for more than $600,000 each!

At car shows, muscle car fans get to see classic muscle cars. They also see the new generation at the same time. The new muscle cars are awesome machines, but nothing beats the power and style of a classic muscle car.

Glossary

Big Three—a term used to describe the largest American automakers; they are Chrysler, Ford, and General Motors.

combustion chamber—the end of a cylinder where fuel is burned

cylinders—hollow chambers inside an engine in which fuel is burned to create power

design cues—the visual features of a car, which are often similar to older, classic models

drive shaft—a mechanism that sends power from the engine to the wheels in a vehicle

engineer—a person who designs machines

fuel efficiency—how much fuel a car uses when driven; a car with poor fuel efficiency requires a lot of fuel.

Hemi—a famous engine developed by Chrysler

large-displacement—refers to an engine with large cylinders in which to burn fuel

mint—like-new condition

power-to-weight ratio—an engine's horsepower divided by the weight of the car it powers

straight-line speed—how fast a car can go in a straight line

torque—a force that turns or twists an object; in the case of a muscle car, torque turns the drive shaft, which turns the rear wheels.

V8—an engine with eight fuel-burning cylinders arranged in the shape of a "V"

To Learn More

AT THE LIBRARY

Bailey, Katharine. *Muscle Cars*. New York, N.Y.: Crabtree, 2006.

Poolos, J. *Wild About Muscle Cars*. New York, N.Y.: PowerKids Press, 2007.

Zuehlke, Jeffrey. *Muscle Cars*. Minneapolis, Minn.: Lerner, 2006.

ON THE WEB

Learning more about muscle cars is as easy as 1, 2, 3.

1. Go to www.factsurfer.com.

2. Enter "muscle cars" into the search box.

3. Click the "Surf" button and you will see a list of related Web sites.

With factsurfer.com, finding more information is just a click away.

Index

The images in this book are reproduced through the courtesy of: Ron Kimball / KimballStock, front cover, pp. 4-5, 6-7, 8-9, 10-11, 12 (top), 12-13, 14-15; Niklas Johansson, pp. 16-17; Digital 94086, pp. 18-19; Jdebordphoto, pp. 20-21.